EXCEL FORMULAS AND FUNCTIONS

Your Step-by-Step Guide to Effective Financial Analysis and Business Modeling

Dave Wright

TABLE OF CONTENTS

Introduction

The Microsoft Excel application is a spreadsheet containing separate cells that can be utilized to build graphs, tables, formulas and functions that easily analyze and organize large amounts of data and information. Excel operates like a database, organized into columns (represented by letters) and rows (represented by numbers) that contain functions, formulas, and information used to execute complex calculations. Excel is a universal application found on almost every business and personal computer in the world.

Why use Excel?

Excel is the simplest way to manage and organize financial information, hence why several businesses use it extensively. It provides total customization and flexibility in the way it is used. Accessibility is another reason to use Excel. With practically no experience or training, a user can create a workbook, start entering data and begin analyzing and calculating information. The main reasons to use Excel are:

- For calculations.
- To organize personal information.

- To organize employee information.
- To organize contact information.
- To organize financial data.

Functions and formulas are the foundation for performing calculations in Excel. This book will help you to know and work with the most essential formulas, functions, and shortcuts for an effective financial analysis and business modeling.

Chapter 1

Basic Excel Terms

Workbook — this is an Excel spreadsheet file. It contains all the data entered and enables you to calculate or sort the results. Shared Workbook is one that is viewed and edited by several users on a network.

Worksheet — this is also referred to as spreadsheet and is a document within the workbook. Multiple worksheets can exist in a workbook. Tabs at the lower portion of the workbook will indicate the active worksheets.

Ribbon — this is a section hosting command tabs, and is at the top of the workbook. Each tab in the Ribbon contains various options to meet your needs.

Template — this is a formatted worksheet or workbook designed to help users meet a specific requirement in Excel. Examples include calendar, process map, and stock analysis.

Cell — this is a rectangular box with which to enter data.

Columns and Rows — these refers to how the cells are aligned. Rows are aligned horizontally while columns are aligned vertically.

Cell Reference — this is a set of coordinates used to identify a particular cell. It is a combination of numbers and letters. For example, B7 would identify the cell located where column B and row 7 intersect.

Cell Range — this is a group of cells recognized as a collection based on multiple criteria. Excel determines the array or range when a colon (:) is used between cell references. For example, A2:C2, tells Excel to examine the cells in the row between A2 and C2, while D3:G8 tells excel to examine the cells within columns D to G and rows 3 to 8. A 3-D reference has to do with a range that covers more than one worksheet residing in the same workbook.

AutoFormat — this is an automatic format applied to cells that meet pre-determined criteria. It could be as easy as font size and alignment.

AutoFill — this enables effortless copying of data across more than one cell.

Cell Formatting — this involves making changes to the visual appearance of cell data in the spreadsheet.

Conditional Formatting — this only applies formatting when the cell satisfies determined criteria such as values below or above a threshold, or duplicate values.

Merged Cell — this is when more than one cells are combined.

Operator — these are signs or symbols that indicates how the calculation will be done in an expression.

Error Code — this appears if Excel finds an issue with a provided formula.

Filter — these are rules used to decide on the rows to display in a worksheet. It can use data like values or conditions.

Freeze Panes — this enables you to select certain columns and/or rows to stay visible on the worksheet.

Chapter 2

Mathematical Operators

Standard operators in Excel are:

Operator	Symbol	Example
( )	Parenthesis	=(1+5)/2=6
^	Exponent	=2^3=8
/	Division	=4/2=2
*	Multiplication	=4*5=20
-	Subtraction	=5-2=3
+	Addition	=8+3=11

Logical Operators

These operators offer support for comparisons such as "less than", "greater than", etc. Below are the logical operators in Excel:

Sign	Condition	Example	Description
=	Equal to	=B1=5	Returns TRUE if the value in cell B1 equals 5, FALSE otherwise.
<>	Not equal to	=B1<>5	Returns TRUE if the value in cell B1 does not equal 5, FALSE

Sign	Condition	Example	Description
			otherwise.
<	Less than	=B1<50	Returns TRUE if the value in cell B1 is less than 50, FALSE otherwise.
<=	Lees than or equal to	=B1<=42	Returns TRUE if the value in cell B1 is less than or equal to 42, FALSE otherwise.
>	Greater than	=B1>50	Returns TRUE if the value in cell B1 is greater than 50, FALSE otherwise.
>=	Greater than or equal to	=B1>=89	Returns TRUE if the value in cell B1 is greater than or equal to 89, FALSE otherwise.

Order of Operations

A mathematical expression with a single operator, such as 3+6 is a simple formula. A complex formula includes more than a single mathematical operator, such as 2+7*4. On such occasions where the formula contains more than one operator, the order of operations informs Excel which operation to solve first. In order to utilize Excel to calculate complicated formulas, you will have to know the order of operations. Excel calculates formulas by using the subsequent order of operations:

- Parentheses.
- Exponential calculations (for example, 2^5).
- Multiplication and division, whichever first shows up.
- Addition and subtraction, whichever first shows up.
- Concatenation &.
- Logical operators.

Chapter 3

Formulas

In Excel, a formula can be referred to as an expression that works on values in a particular cell or a range of cells. For instance, =C1+C2+C3, returns the total of the range of cell values from cell C1 to cell C3. As shown below where cell C4 contains the sum of C1, C2 and C3.

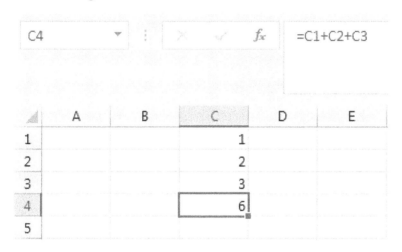

Enter a Formula

Below are the steps to enter a formula:

- Choose a cell.
- Every formula in Excel must start with an equals sign (=).

- Type the formula (use the example above), and then press Enter.

Note: Excel automatically calculates any changes in the value in any of the cells, C1 to C3.

Edit a Formula

There are three ways to edit a formula

- Click on the cell, press F2, and edit.
- Double-click on the cell, and edit.
- Click on the cell, and modify in the formula bar.

For any option chose, make sure to press Enter when done, in order for the changes to be confirmed. If you change your mind and no longer want to change the formula, press the Escape (Esc) key on the keyboard.

Understanding Cell References

It is important to use cell references so that values can be automatically updated as needed. Using hardcoded values is regarded as bad form because there will not be any change in the results unless you manually change the value or formula again. Hardcoding values also hides information and make it more difficult to maintain a spreadsheet. Examples below will explain this better.

Hardcoded values:

Cell A1 contains the result of 5+7. Only manual updates can be done here.

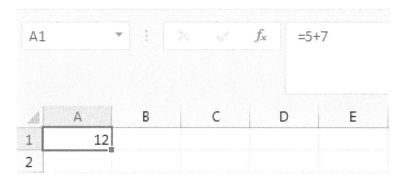

Using cell references:

Cell C1 point to the sum of the cell references instead of values.

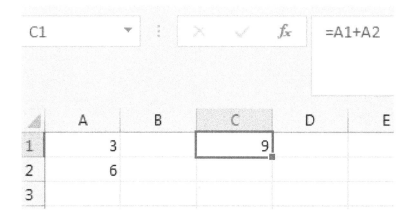

Copying a formula to a new location, causes the cell references to be automatically updated. Meaning that there is no need to fill in the same formula repeatedly. Below, cell E1 shows the sum of B1, C1 and D1

E1	▾ ⋮	✕ ✓	f_x	=B1+C1+D1

◢	A	B	C	D	E
1	Desk	56	45	14	115
2	Chair	76	23	13	
3	Notebook	12	65	10	
4					

Copy the formula in E1 (press Ctrl + C) and paste in E2 (press Ctrl +V). You will notice the change in references.

E2	▾ ⋮	✕ ✓	f_x	=B2+C2+D2

◢	A	B	C	D	E
1	Desk	56	45	14	115
2	Chair	76	23	13	112
3	Notebook	12	65	10	
4					

Do the same for E3. Cell addresses are changed again.

| E3 | ▾ | ⋮ | ✕ | ✓ | f_x | =B3+C3+D3 |

◢	A	B	C	D	E
1	Desk	56	45	14	115
2	Chair	76	23	13	112
3	Notebook	12	65	10	87

Absolute and Relative References

The cell references described above are referred to as relative references. Denoting that the reference points to a range of cells or a particular cell. When copied across several cells, they change depending on the relative location of columns and rows. For instance, if the formula =B1+C1+D1 is copied from the first row to the second row, the formula becomes =B2+C2+D2. Relative references are especially useful whenever there is need to repeat same calculation across several rows or columns.

For times when it is not needed for a cell reference to update when copied to additional cells, use an absolute reference. Absolute references doesn't get changed when filled or copied. It can be used to keep a column or row constant. To make a cell reference absolute, make use of the dollar sign ($). This sign can precede the row reference, the column reference, or both. When entering a formula, use the F4 key to switch between absolute and relative cell references.

For example, as shown below, every value in column D is multiplied by the value in A1, which is 10. Having A1 as an absolute reference "locks" that reference so that it does not change even after the formula has been copied to E2 and E3.

Formula in E2 becomes =D2*A1
Formula in E3 becomes =D3*A1

E1	▼ ⋮	✕ ✓ f_x	=D1*A1	
	A	B	C	D	E
1	5		Purple	3	15
2			Orange	4	20
3			Red	8	40

From the above, it can be seen that the reference to A1 never changes. When A1 value is manually updated, all the formulas referencing it will automatically recalculate.

Using the same example, we will change the value of A1 to 8 to see how it gets updated.

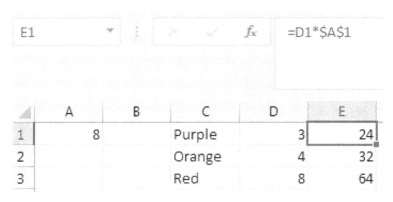

After understanding cell references, it makes more sense not to hardcode values in a formula. Since saving the value in A1, and referring to it with an absolute reference, makes sure that the value can be updated as needed and all related formulas will change immediately.

Results from a Formula

In Excel, every formula shows a result, regardless of it is an error or not. For example, in cell D4 below, the result is an error (#DIV/0!) since B4 is empty. D2 and D3 returns correct result. When this is noticed, you can either update B4 with the missing error or utilize the IFERROR function to catch that error. This function will be discussed in more detail in subsequent chapters.

D4			✗	✓	f_x	=(C4-B4)/B4

	A	B	C	D	E
1	Fruit	Bought	Sold	Percentage	
2	Mango	$300	$350	16.67%	
3	Apple	$120	$180	50.00%	
4	Banana		◈ 0	#DIV/0!	
5					

Convert Formulas to Values

There are times when you want to remove formulas, and leave only values instead. To accomplish this, copy the formula, and paste, right-click and select Paste Special > Values. This way, the formula is overwritten with the values it return. You can make use of a keyboard shortcut, or use the Paste options in the Home tab on the Excel ribbon.

Chapter 4

Functions

"Formula" and "function" are words used frequently in Excel, at times interchangeably. They are somehow related, but not really the same. In principle, a formula is an expression that starts with an equals sign (=). On the other hand, a function is a predetermined formula that performs calculations by utilizing particular values in a specific order. In most instances, functions have names that indicate their intended use. The correct usage of functions requires an understanding of the different aspects of a function and the creation of arguments to compute values and cell references.

Aspects of a Function

For a function to work correctly, it should be written in a particular way, called the syntax. The straightforward syntax for a function contains the equals sign (=), the name of the function (for example, SUM), and one or more than one arguments. Arguments contain the data you want to calculate. For example, the function =SUM(B1:B10) adds the values in the cell range B1 to B10.

Function Arguments

Arguments involves both cell ranges and individual cells, which must be enclosed inside parentheses. You can include multiple arguments or one argument, depending on the syntax needed for the function. For instance, the function =AVERAGE(A1:A10) would compute the average of the total values within the cell range A1:A10. This function has only one argument.

A11	▼ :	✕ ✓ *fx*	=AVERAGE(A1:A10)

	A	B	C	D	E
1	6				
2	7				
3	9				
4	27				
5	46				
6	87				
7	29				
8	12				
9	41				
10	50				
11	=AVERAGE(A1:A10)				

A comma must separate multiple arguments. For instance, the function =SUM(A1:A4, C1:C3, E1:E2) will add the values of every cell in the three arguments.

A6	▾	⋮	✕	✓	*fₓ*	=SUM(A1:A4,C1:C3,E1:E2)

	A	B	C	D	E	F
1	6		4		7	
2	9		5		9	
3	3		8			
4	2					
5						
6	=SUM(A1:A4,C1:C3,E1:E2)					

Inserting Functions

- **Manually enter a function**

  Entering a formula in the formula bar or a cell is the most direct method of inserting simple Excel formulas. The process typically starts by inputting an equal sign, and then the function's name. Excel has made this easier, such that when you start entering the function's name, it shows a pop-up function hint. You can select your preference from this list. However, do not press the Enter key. Rather, press the Tab key to continue to insert other choices. If not, you may come across an invalid name error, mostly depicted as '#NAME?'. To resolve it, just select the cell again, and click on the formulas tab to complete your function.

- **AutoSum option**
  The AutoSum function is a convenient option for quickly completing everyday tasks. To use this, go to the Home tab, at the far-right corner, select the AutoSum option. This will show a dropdown of other hidden formulas. You can also find this in the Formulas tab; it is the second option right after Insert Function.

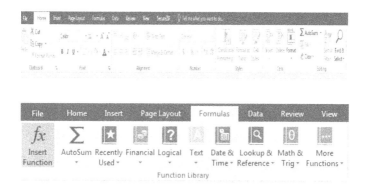

- **Through the Insert Function selection in Formulas tab**
  For complete control when inserting functions, use the Insert Function dialogue box. To do this, select the Formulas tab and click on the first option named Insert Function. The pop-up dialogue box will have all the functions needed to finish your financial analysis.

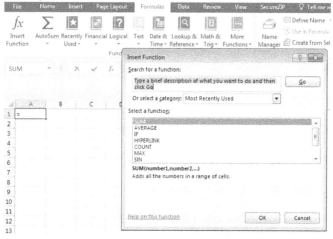

- **Choose a formula from any of the clusters in Formula tab**
This choice is for those who need to use their favorite functions rapidly. To do this, go to the Formulas bar and choose your desired group. Click on the option to show a sub-menu containing a list of functions. After which, you can choose your preference. If your desired group is not displayed on the tab, select the More Functions option –it is probably just hidden there.

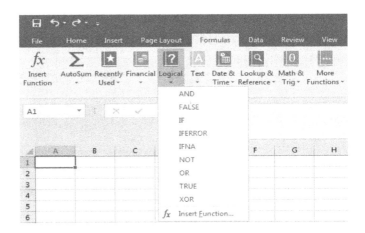

- **Quick insert: through Recently Used option**
  If it becomes tedious or repetitive to re-type your most recent formula, you can utilize the Recently Used option. You can find it on the Formulas tab; it is the third option right after AutoSum.

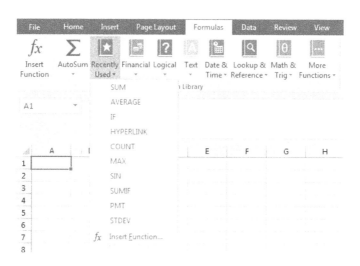

Chapter 5

Basic Excel Functions to Know

Since you are now able to insert and edit your preferred function and formulas correctly, let us look into some basic Excel functions to start with.

- **MIN and MAX**

  The MIN and MAX functions are under the Excel Statistical functions category. MIN will return the smallest value from a specified set of numeric values. The MIN function is used in financial modeling for calculating depreciation schedules and debt schedules.

  MAX will return the largest value from a specified set of numeric values. The MAX function is used in financial modeling for calculating the highest revenue amount or expense, the fastest time, the highest score, etc.

  The MIN and MAX functions both ignores logical values (FALSE/TRUE), text and numbers.

  Formula
  =MIN(number1, [number2], ...)

=MAX(number1, [number2], ...)

Here, the arguments utilized for the MIN and MAX functions are number1 and number2, where number1 is mandatory and the following values are optional. In the 2007 and later versions of Excel, up to 255 number arguments can be provided to the MIN/MAX function. For 2003 and earlier versions of Excel, only a maximum of 30 number arguments is accepted.

Arguments can be given as cell ranges, cell references, or constants. If the argument in the MIN/MAX function is a range of cells or a cell reference, it will ignore logical values or text and empty cells that are within the cell range. However, text representations of numbers and logical values that are entered directly into the function will not be ignored.

Example for MIN function
=MIN(B3:B6) – Finds the minimum number between the values in the cell range B3 to B6.

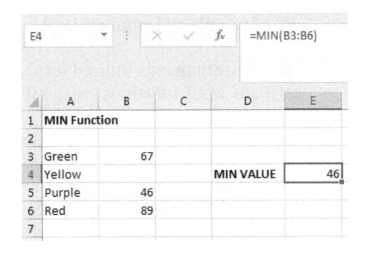

Example for MAX function

=MAX(B3:B6) – Finds the largest number between the values in the cell range B3 to B6.

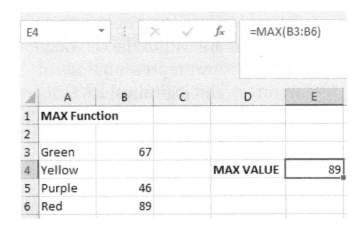

Note that the empty values above was ignored by both the MIN and MAX functions. In addition, you get the error "#VALUE!" if there are non-numeric values in the MIN/MAX function.

- **COUNT**
  The COUNT Function is under the Excel Statistical functions category. This function assists in counting the total number of cells that has a number, along with the total number of arguments that have numbers. The function also counts numbers in any specified range. This was made available in Excel in 2000. The COUNT function is used in financial modeling to analyze data, to record the number of cells in a specified range.

  Formula
  =COUNT(value1, value2....)

  Here, value1 is a required argument while value2 is optional. Up to 255 arguments can be provided to the COUNT function. Only numbers will be counted and everything else ignored.

Example

	A	B	C	D	E
					=COUNT(B3:B6)
1	COUNT Function				
2					
3	Green	67			
4	Yellow	43		COUNT	4
5	Purple	46			
6	Red	89			
7					

E4 — =COUNT(B3:B6)

- **COUNTA**

   The COUNTA Function is under the Excel Statistical functions category. It will calculate the total number of cells that contains value (are not empty) within a specified set of values. This function can also be known as the COUNTIF Not Blank function. It is useful for financial analysis for recording the number of cells in a specified range.

   Formula
   =COUNTA(value1, [value2], ...)
   Here, value1 is a required argument while value2 is optional. Up to 255

arguments can be provided to the COUNTA function. Value arguments can be cell references, cell ranges or cell values. Unlike the COUNT function that evaluates only numbers, COUNTA evaluates errors, logical values, text values, dates and numbers.

Example

E5		▼ : × ✓	f_x	=COUNTA(B3:B9)

◢	A	B	C	D	E
1	COUNTA Function				
2					
3	Green	67			
4		FALSE			
5	Yellow	43		COUNT	6
6		#DIV/0!			
7					
8	Purple	46			
9	Red	89			

- **AVERAGE**
  The AVERAGE function is under the Excel Statistical functions category. It will provide the average of a particular sequence of numbers. In financial analysis, this function is used to get the

mean/average of a sequence of numbers. For example, to calculate the average sales over the last 12 months.

Formula
=AVERAGE(number1, [number2], ...)
Here, number1 is a required argument while number2 is optional. Up to 255 arguments can be provided to the AVERAGE function. The function ignores blank cells. If a cell reference or range argument contains empty cells, logical values, or text, those values are ignored. Nevertheless, cells that have zero as the value are included. Text or error values arguments that cannot be converted to numbers lead to errors in the function.

Example

E4			×	✓	f_x	=AVERAGE(B3:B6)

▲	A	B	C	D	E
1	AVERAGE Function				
2					
3	Green	67			
4	Yellow	43		AVERAGE	61.25
5	Purple	46			
6	Red	89			

- **SUM**

  The SUM function is under the Math and Trigonometry functions category. The function will add all the cell values that are provided as numerous arguments. This function is widely used and very popular in Excel. SUM helps users carry out a quick summation of itemized cells. For example, we can utilize the function to calculate the total cost of items purchased for an event.

  Formula
  =SUM(number1, [number2], [number3]......)

  Here, number1 and number2 are required arguments, number3 and subsequent arguments are optional. Up to 255 arguments can be provided to the SUM function. Arguments can be provided as constants, arrays, ranges, cell references, numbers, and the outputs of other functions or formulas.

Example

	A	B	C	D	E
	E4	▾ : × ✓ fx		=SUM(B3:B6)	

	A	B	C	D	E
1	SUM Function				
2					
3	Green	67			
4	Yellow	43		SUM	245
5	Purple	46			
6	Red	89			

- **TRIM**

  The TRIM function is under the Excel Text functions category. TRIM assists in removing the additional spaces in data and therefore cleaning up the cells within the worksheet. The TRIM function is used in financial analysis to remove irregular spacing from data brought in from other applications.

  Formula
  =TRIM(text)

  Here, the text is a required argument, from which we can remove the extra spaces. The removal of extra spaces from the text will lead to words having only single spaces between them, and there would be no space character at either the end or beginning of the text. TRIM is very convenient when tidying up text from other environments or applications. Only the ASCII space character(32) is removed from the text. The non-breaking space character (160) of a Unicode text that shows up as an HTML entity in web pages will not be resolved by TRIM.

Example

| B2 | ▼ | : | × | ✓ | *fx* | =TRIM(A2) |

◢	A	B
1	Raw Data	TRIM
2	Having too many	Having too many
3	spaces in a given	spaces in a given
4	sentence is not ideal	sentence is not ideal

- **IF**
  The Excel IF Statement checks a given condition and provide one value for a FALSE result and a different value for a TRUE result. For example, if total sales is more than $1000, then output a "Yes" for Incentive – Else, return a "No" for

Incentive. The IF function can also be used to evaluate a particular function, or include numerous IF functions in a single formula. In Excel, multiple IF statements are referred to as nested IF statements. The IF function is used in financial analysis to analyze and evaluate data by assessing specific conditions. The function evaluates errors, values and text.

Formula
=IF(logical_test, value_if_true, value_if_false)

Here, logical_test is a required argument, and is the condition to be assessed as either FALSE or TRUE. Value_if_true is an optional argument, and is the value returned if logical_test is assessed as TRUE. Value_if_false is an optional argument, and is the value returned if logical_test is assessed as FALSE. Logical operators can also be used when utilizing the IF function to create a test.

Example

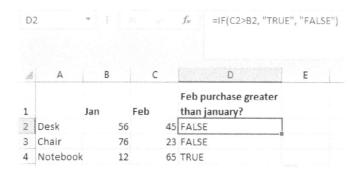

- **VALUE**

  The VALUE Function is under the Excel Text functions category. It converts a text string representation of a number into a plain number. Therefore, it converts text that are in a recognized format (time, date, or number format) to a numeric value. This function is not utilized as much for financial analysis. Since Excel automatically transforms texts to numbers. Nonetheless, it is essential for all who wants to know the full extent of functions in Excel.

  Formula
  =VALUE(Text)

The text here can be either inside quotes or points to a cell that have the text to be converted. It is a required argument.

Example

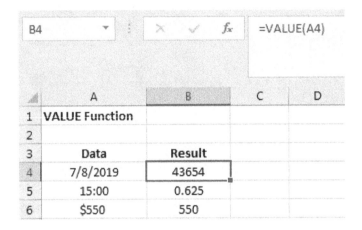

From the above, VALUE function converts the date, time and amount into number formats.

Chapter 6

Advanced Excel Functions

Below are the most essential and advanced Excel functions that every topnotch financial analyst must know.

- **Concatenate**

  The CONCATENATE Function is under the Excel Text functions category. The function assists in combining more than one strings into a single string. Data is often handled during financial analysis, but most times that data is not in a good enough format for analysis and might create a need for multiple cells to be merged, or the splitting of data from one cell to several cells. The concatenate function aids in achieving that.

  Formula
  =CONCATENATE(text1, [text2], ...)

  Here, text1 and text2 are required arguments, and they are items to join. These items can be a number, cell reference or text value. The function can accommodate a maximum of 255 arguments that have up to 8192 characters.

Example

Formulas used

=CONCATENATE(A3," ",B3)
=CONCATENATE(A4,", ",B4)
=CONCATENATE(A5," - ",B5)
=CONCATENATE(A6," & ",B6)

D3		:	×	✓	f_x	=CONCATENATE(A3," ",B3)

◢	A	B	C	D	E	F
1	Concatenate Function					
2				Result		
3	Red	Plum		Red Plum		
4	Green	White		Green, White		
5	Yellow	Orange		Yellow - Orange		
6	Blue	Purple		Blue & Purple		
7						

- **CHOOSE**

  The CHOOSE function is under the Lookup and Reference functions category. It returns a value from a cell range that corresponds to the given index number. The CHOOSE function will provide the nth item in a given list. It is used in financial analysis to create scenarios in financial models. Using this function, an analyst can choose between multiple scenarios that can flow across the whole model. Scenario analysis is one essential aspect of constructing a robust financial model.

Formula
=CHOOSE(index_num, value1, [value2], ...)

Here, index_num is a required argument. It is an integer that identifies which value argument is chosen. It can be either a cell reference, or a number that is between 1 and 254, or a formula. Value1 is a required argument, but subsequent values are optional. The output should be from a list of values (one or more).

Notes:
  o If index_num is a cell range, CHOOSE will evaluate all values.
  o If index_num happens to be a fraction, it gets truncated to the smallest integer before it is used.
  o Value1 and value2 has to be entered as separate values (or references to separate cells containing values.
  o If index_num is 1, the CHOOSE function returns value1; if the

index_num is 2, the CHOOSE
function returns value2; and so
forth.

- o #NAME? error – takes place when
  value arguments are invalid cell
  references or are text values not
  enclosed in quotes.
- o VALUE! error – takes place when:
  Provided index_num argument is
  non-numeric.
  Provided index_num is greater
  than the specified number of
  values or is less than 1.

Example
Formulas used
=CHOOSE(A4,"red","blue","green")
=CHOOSE(A5,"red","blue","green")
=CHOOSE(A6,"red","blue","green")

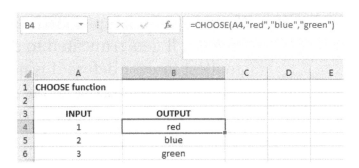

- **INDEX MATCH**
  This is an advanced substitute to the HLOOKUP or VLOOKUP functions (which have several limitations and drawbacks). The INDEX MATCH function combines two Excel functions, which are INDEX and MATCH.

  =INDEX() gets a cell value in a list based on the row and column number. =MATCH() gets the location of an item in a column or row.

  Combined, both formulas can find and get a cell value in a list based on horizontal and vertical criteria.

  Example (INDEX function only)
  Using the table below as a guide, we will utilize the INDEX function to find out how many chairs were bought in February. Follow these steps
    o Write "=INDEX(" and select the entire table and add a comma.
    o Write the row number for Chair, which is "3" then add a comma.
    o Write the column number for Feb, which is "3" then close the bracket.
    o The result is "23".

| D3 | ▾ | ⋮ | ✕ | ✓ | *fx* | =INDEX(A1:C4,3,3) |

◢	A	B	C	D	E
1	Item	Jan	Feb		
2	Desk	56	45		
3	Chair	76	23	23	
4	Notebook	12	65		

Example (MATCH function only)

Using the same table as above, we will utilize the MATCH function to look up the row and column number for Chair. To find the row number for Chair, do these

- o Type "=MATCH(" and connect to the cell where "Chair" is in (this is the criteria we are searching for). In this case, A7. Add a comma.
- o Select the every cell in the Item column (including the "Item" header). Add a comma.
- o Type in zero "0" to get an exact match. Then close the bracket.
- o The output is that Chair is in row "3".

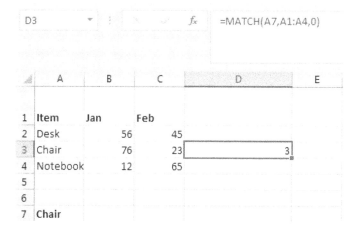

To find the column number for Feb, do these

- o Type "=MATCH(" and connect to the cell where "Feb" is in (this is the criteria we are searching for). In this case, A7. Add a comma.
- o Select every cell across the header row. Add a comma.
- o Type in zero "0" to get an exact match. Then close the bracket.
- o The output is that Feb is in column "3".

| D3 | ▼ | ⋮ | × | ✓ | *fx* | =MATCH(A7,A1:C1,0) |

◢	A	B	C	D	E
1	Item	Jan	Feb		
2	Desk	56	45		
3	Chair	76	23	3	
4	Notebook	12	65		
5					
6					
7	Feb				

Example (Combine INDEX and MATCH):

The original INDEX formula we used is =INDEX(A1:C4,3,3). Now, we are going to replace the last two values in the formula(3,3) with the two MATCH formulas we used above for finding row and column number. This will lead to a INDEX MATCH MATCH function.
Steps below:

- o Copy the MATCH function for Chair and replace the first "3" in the index function with it.
- o Copy the MATCH formula for Feb and replace the second "3" in the index function with it

- The output is that the number of Chairs purchased in February is "23".
- This is now a dynamic INDEX MATCH function.

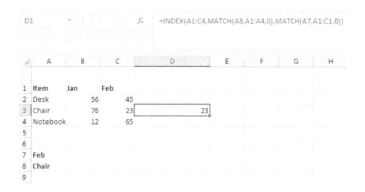

- **PMT and IPMT**
These two functions are combined together in order to separate interest and principal payments.

PMT
The PMT function is under the financial Excel functions category. The function assists in calculating the total payment (interest and principal) required to settle an investment or a loan having a fixed interest rate across a specific period.
Formula

=PMT(rate, nper, pv, [fv], [type])

Here

- The rate, which is the interest rate for the loan, is a required argument.
- Nper, which is the entire amount of payments for the loan, is a required argument.
- Pv, which is the total amount or present value that a series of payments in the future is worth now, is a required argument. It is also referred to as the loan principal.
- Fv, which is the cash balance or future value to be gotten after making the last payment, is an optional argument. If fv is not present, then the default value is zero, meaning that the loan's future value will be zero.
- Type, which refers to the kind of day count basis utilized, is an optional argument. Below are potential values of the basis:

Basis	Day count basis
0 or omitted	US(NASD) 30/360

Basis	Day count basis
1	Actual/actual
2	Actual/360
3	Actual/365
4	European 30/360

Note:
- o #NUM! error – Occurs when: Provided nper value is equals 0. Provided rate value is less than or equal to -1.
- o #VALUE! error – Occurs when there are non-numeric arguments provided.
- o When calculating quarterly or monthly payments, convert the number of periods or annual interest rates to quarters or months.
- o To get the total amount paid for the loan period, multiply the PMT function as calculated by nper.

Example (PMT)
Let us assume that we are investing in such a way that, we will receive $40,000 after one year. The interest rate is 2.99%

per annum and payments will be done at the beginning of each month.

	fx	=PMT(B3/12,B4,B5)

	A	B	C	D	E
1	PMT Function				
2					
3	Interest rate	2.99%			
4	nper	12		Monthly investments	($3,387.57)
5	pv	$40,000			
6	fv				
7	type				

From the above, the PMT function returns $3,387.57, which is the cash outflow per month to realize $40,000 in one year.

- o Since the payments will be made per month, the annual interest rate is changed to a monthly rate. The year was also converted into months, so instead of putting 1 year, it was replaced with 12 months.
- o To show that payments will be done at the start of each month, set type argument to 1.
- o Positive numbers represents incoming payments and negative numbers represents outgoing

payments, according to the common cash flow convention.

- o Since the value above is negative, it shows that an outgoing payment will be made.
- o The value 3,387.57 includes the interest and principal but no fees, reserve payments, or taxes.

IPMT

The IPMT function is under the Excel Financial functions category. It calculates the interest based on a specified loan payment and payment duration. Using IPMT, we can calculate the payment's interest amount for the first duration, last period, or any time in between.

Formula

=IPMT(rate, per, nper, pv, [fv], [type])

Here,

- o Rate – the interest for each period. It is a required argument.
- o Per – the period needed to evaluate the interest, must be within the range 1 to nper. It is a required argument.

- Pv – the lump sum amount or present value, that a series of payments in the future is worth now. It is a required argument.
- Fv – the cash balance or future value to be gotten after making the last payment. It is an optional argument. If fv is not present, then the default value is zero, meaning that the loan's future value will be zero.
- Type – accepts either 1 or 0, and shows when payments are due. If type is not present, then the default value is zero. Type should be set to zero if payments are made towards the end of the payment period, or set to 1 for payments done at the beginning of the period.

Example

We will utilize the IPMT function to get the monthly interest of a $50,000 loan that has to be fully paid in five years. Interest rate is 5% per annum and the loan payment is to be done at the end of every month.

Formula is =IPMT(B4/12,1,B6,B3)

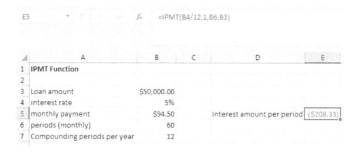

From the above, the monthly interest payments (208.33) is negative, showing that it is an outgoing payment.

- **LEFT, MID, RIGHT, and CELL**
  These functions can be merged to construct complex and advanced formulas to use.

  LEFT
  The LEFT Function is under the Excel TEXT functions category. It will return a specified amount of characters from the beginning of a provided text string. It is used in financial analysis to get characters from the left part of a text. Usually, it is utilized by merging it with other functions like DAY, DATE, COUNT, SUM, VALUE, etc.

Formula
=LEFT(text,[num_chars])

Here, text is the initial text string and is a required argument. num_chars defines the number of characters that should be extracted, beginning from the left part of the text. It is an optional argument. The default value is 1, If num_chars is not provided.

Example
We will extract three characters starting from the left part of the text. First formula is =LEFT(A5,3)

| B5 | ▼ | ⋮ | ✕ | ✓ | *fx* | =LEFT(A5,3) |

◢	A	B	C	D
1	LEFT Function			
2				
3				
4	Data	Result		
5	Computers	Com		
6	Laptops	Lap		
7	Desktops	Des		
8	Towers	Tow		

MID

The MID function is under the Excel
TEXT functions category. It will return a
specified amount of characters from the
center of a provided text string. . It is
used in financial analysis to get
characters from the center part of a text.
Usually, it is utilized by merging it with
other functions like DAY, DATE,
COUNT, SUM, VALUE, etc.

Formula
=MID(text, start_num, num_chars)

Here, text is the initial text string and is
a required argument. Start_num is an
integer that specifies the location of the
first character to be returned.
Num_chars identifies the number of
characters, beginning with start_num,
that should be returned from the
beginning of the given text.

Example
The first formula is =MID(A4,B4,C4)

| D4 | ▼ | : | × | ✓ | fx | =MID(A4,B4,C4) |

▲	A	B	C	D
1	MID Function			
2				
3	Data	Start	Char	Result
4	An example to check	4	4	exam
5	how long the total	6	2	on
6	length per row will be	17	3	ill

RIGHT

The RIGHT Function is under the Excel TEXT functions category. It will return a given amount of characters from the right part of a specified text string. It is used in financial analysis to get characters from the right portion of a text string. Usually, it is utilized by merging it with other functions like DAY, DATE, COUNT, SUM, VALUE, etc.

Formula
=RIGHT(text,[num_chars])

Example
We will extract five characters starting from the right part of the text. First formula is =RIGHT(A5,5)

	A	B	C	D
			=RIGHT(A5,5)	
1	RIGHT Function			
2				
3				
4	Data	Result		
5	Computers	uters		
6	Laptops	ptops		
7	Desktops	ktops		
8	Towers	owers		

CELL

The CELL function is under the Excel Information function category. It extracts information about a cell's formatting, contents, or location. The CELL function have two arguments, one that defines the information type to be gotten and the other denotes the cell to check. It is used in financial analysis to validate that a cell holds numeric value rather than text, before calculations are done. If data is imported from an external source, this function can be used to verify its format.

Formula
=CELL(info_type, [reference])

Here, reference is the cell to check for and is an optional argument. If a cell range is provided, the returned information corresponds to the cell range's top left cell. If there is no reference, the returned information corresponds to the most recent cell that was changed. Info_type is the text value defining the information type to be returned. This can be any of the following:

Info_type	Description
Format	Returns a code that matches the cell's number format.
Contents	Returns the value of the reference's upper-left cell. Does not return formulas, instead, it returns the output of the formula.
Width	Returns column's width.
Row	Returns a cell's row number.

Prefix	Returns a text value matching the cell's "label prefix".
Address	Returns the location of a reference's first cell as text.
Protect	Returns 1 for locked cell, else 0.
Parentheses	Returns 1 if the reference's first cell has parentheses, else 0.
Col	Returns column number of a reference's first cell.
Filename	Returns full path and file name as text. If it is an unsaved worksheet (containing the reference), an empty string is supplied.
Color	Returns 1 if the reference's first cell has a color for

	negative values, else 0.
Type	Returns a text value matching the cell's data type. It can either be "l" for label (specifically text constant), "b" for blank, or "v" for value (intended for any other type of data).

Example
To get the location of a lookup result gotten through the INDEX function, utilize the CELL function.

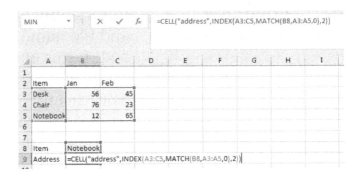

The INDEX function will show the cell's value at a specified index, but the function beneath it essentially returns a reference. Therefore, by enclosing INDEX within the CELL function, the cell's address is returned by the lookup.

This is shown below:

| B9 | | | f_x | =CELL("address",INDEX(A3:C5,MATCH(B8,A3:A5,0),2)) |

	A	B	C	D	E	F	G	H	I
1									
2	Item	Jan	Feb						
3	Desk	56	45						
4	Chair	76	23						
5	Notebook	12	65						
6									
7									
8	Item	Notebook							
9	Address	B5							

- **LEN**
  The LEN Function is under the Excel TEXT functions category. The function will get the length of a specified text string. The LEN function is used in financial analysis to return the length of a specified test string, that is, it returns the number of characters. Also, it will count the characters in numbers, but does not include number formatting.

  Formula
  =LEN(text)

Here, text is what we need to calculate the length, and it is required argument. This text argument can be provided either directly, or as a pointer to a cell having a string, or as a string gotten from another function.

Example

B4		:	✕	✓	f_x	=LEN(A4)

◢	A	B	C	D
1	LEN Function			
2				
3	Data	Length		
4	An example to check	19		
5	how long the total	18		
6	length per row will be	22		
7		0		
8	Done	4		

From the above it can be seen that spaces in the text are also counted as characters. The length of the blank row or empty string in cell A7 is 0.

Let us look at another example. Here, the LEN function will be utilized to remove characters. We would remove the last 5 characters in each row. LEFT and LEN functions can be used together to remove the preceding n characters from a string. Below, we will be removing miles from the data, which is the last 5 characters.

Formula used is
=VALUE(LEFT(A4,LEN(A4)-6))

B4					f_x	=VALUE(LEFT(A4,LEN(A4)-6))

	A	B	C	D	E
1	LEN Function				
2					
3	Data	Result			
4	1289 miles	1289			
5	535 miles	535			
6	7642 miles	7642			
7	8964 miles	8964			
8	3821 miles	3821			

In the example above, the LEFT function extracted characters from the left part of the specified value. Then the LEN function calculated the total length of every value. To find out the amount of characters to extract, we subtracted 6 – this is the total length of " miles" (the space character is included as well). Using cell B4 as an example, after subtracting 6, the remainder is 4, which is passed to LEFT as the total number of characters to extract. Then LEFT returns the text "1289" as a text value. We used VALUE function since it converts numbers in text value formats to plain numbers.

- **OFFSET combined with AVERAGE or SUM**
  We will first explain the OFFSET function before showing how it works in combination with SUM or AVERAGE. The OFFSET function is under the Lookup and Reference functions category. It returns a range of cells. To be precise, it will return an identified number of columns and rows from the first range that was specified. It is used in financial analysis building a named range for pivot charts or tables to ensure that the data is always current.

  Formula
  = OFFSET(reference, rows, cols, [height], [width])

  Here,
  - o Reference – range of cells to be offset. This can be either one cell

or multiple cells. It is a required argument.

- o Rows – amount of rows from the upper-left (start) of the provided reference, to the beginning of the returned range. This is a required argument.
- o Cols – amount of columns from the upper-left left (start) of the provided reference, to the beginning of the returned range. This is a required argument.
- o Height – height of the returned cell range. When not provided, the returned cell range will have the same height like that of the supplied reference argument. This is an optional argument.
- o Width – width of the returned cell range. When not provided, the returned cell range will have the same width like that of the supplied reference argument. This is an optional argument.

Example

| F5 | ▼ | : | ✕ | ✓ | *fx* | =OFFSET(A3,3,1) |

◢	A	B	C	D	E	F
1	OFFSET Function					
2						
3	Item	Jan	Feb			
4	Desk	56	45			
5	Chair	76	23		RESULT:	12
6	Notebook	12	65			

From the above, using the formula =OFFSET(A3,3,1) , we get 12 as our result, since it is three rows down and one column right after the reference.

Combining OFFSET with SUM

The OFFSET function alone may not necessarily be classified as advanced, but when combined with additional functions like AVERAGE or SUM we can construct a sophisticated formula. Assume we want to build a dynamic function to sum various number of cells. Using just the SUM function, the calculation will be static, but by adding OFFSET to that formula we can move the cell reference. To make this work, the SUM function's ending reference cell will be substituted with the OFFSET function. Thus, making the formula dynamic. The cell referenced in the example below, E2, is where to denote the number of consecutive cells to add up.

Example

| C7 | | | | | f_x | =SUM(B4:OFFSET(B4,0,E2-1)) |

	A	B	C	D	E	F	G
1							
2		Sum this many numbers:			4		
3							
4		6	3	5	7	8	2
5							
6							
7		Solution	21				

From the above, the SUM formula begins in cell B4, but it finishes with a variable, and this is the OFFSET function beginning at B4 and going forward by using the value in E2 ("4"), minus one. Hence, moving the SUM function's end across 2 cells, summing 4 years of data (together with the starting point). As shown in cell C7, the sum of cells B4:E4 is 21, which is what the SUM and OFFSET formula gives us.

- **SUMIF and COUNTIF**
  Both of these advanced functions are great practices of conditional functions.

  SUMIF
  The SUMIF function is under the Math and Trigonometry functions category. This function sums up cells that fulfill the specified criteria. The criteria are centered on text, numbers, and dates. It supports wildcards (*, ?) and also logical operators like (=,>,<,<>). The SUMIF function is frequently used in financial analysis.

  Formula
  =SUMIF(range, criteria, [sum_range])
  Here,
    o Range – range of cells to apply against the criteria. This is a required argument.
    o Criteria – criteria utilized to determine the cells that need to be added. This is a required argument. The criteria can either be an expression (for example, "<>0",">40"), or a text string (for example, "Peach", "Borrow"), or a

numeric value which could be a logical value, time, date, decimal, or integer (for example, TRUE, 40, 08/08/2019).

- o Sum_range – cells that contain numeric values (or array of numeric values) to be added together when the corresponding range entry meets the given criteria. If there is no sum_range argument, the range argument's values are summed instead.

Example

The below example used SUMIF function to find the total number of desks purchased. Criteria that contains math symbols or text criteria must be within double quotation marks (" ").

F7				f_x	=SUMIF(A4:A10,"Desk",B4:B10)		
	A	B	C	D	E	F	G
1	SUMIF Function						
2							
3	Item	Purchases					
4	Desk	56					
5	Chair	76					
6	Notebook	12					
7	Pencil	23		Total Desk Purchased:		184	
8	Desk	37					
9	Notebook	60					
10	Desk	91					

COUNTIF

This counts the amount of cells that fulfill a specific criterion. It is under the Excel Statistical functions category.

Formula
=COUNTIF(Range, criteria)
Here,
- o Range – defines one or multiple cells to count. This will be evaluated against the specified criteria and only gets counted when it meets the criteria. This is a required argument.
- o Criteria –a condition that we define.

Example
Using the same table as above, we will check how many times Desk was mentioned in the table.

	A	B	C	D	E	F
1	SUMIF Function					
2						
3	Item	Purchases				
4	Desk	56				
5	Chair	76				
6	Notebook	12				
7	Pencil	23		Desk Count:	3	
8	Desk	37				
9	Notebook	60				
10	Desk	91				

- ## IF combined with OR/AND

  Nested IF functions can become a nightmare. Merging IF with either the OR or the AND function can be a good way to ensure that formulas are easier to audit and simpler for other users to comprehend.

  ## OR

  The OR Function is under the Excel LOGICAL functions category. It determines if one or more conditions in a test returns TRUE. It is used in financial analysis to compare two values or two statements.

Formula

=OR(logical1, [logical2], ...)

Here,

- o Logical1 – logical value or first condition to evaluate. Required argument.
- o Logical2 – logical value or second condition to evaluate. Optional argument.

Example

Simple OR function demonstration

D4		▼		✕	✓	f_x	=OR(A4>0, A4<B4)

◢	A	B	C	D
1	OR Function			
2				
3	Data 1	Data 2	Formula	Result
4	4	9	OR(A4>0, A4<B4)	TRUE
5	4	9	OR(A5>0,A5>B5,B5>15)	TRUE
6	4	9	OR(A6<0,A6>B6,B6>15)	FALSE

In the above table:

The OR function in cell D4 returns TRUE, since both of the given conditions are TRUE;

The OR function in cell D5 returns TRUE, since the first condition, A4>0 evaluates to TRUE;

The OR function in cell D6 returns FALSE, since all of the given conditions are FALSE.

Example using OR function and IF function

Assume we are provided with student marks and we need the formula to show "PASS" for marks that are above 60 in Literature or above 55 in Philosophy and show "FAIL" for marks that are below it. Note that as long as one condition is met, the function will return PASS.

D4				f_x	=IF(OR(B4>60,C4>55),"PASS","FAIL")		

	A	B	C	D	E	F	G
1	OR and IF Function						
2							
3	Roll number	Marks in Literature	Marks in Philosophy	Result			
4	1	34	23	FAIL			
5	2	56	45	FAIL			
6	3	44	87	PASS			
7	4	75	90	PASS			
8	5	65	57	PASS			
9	6	89	39	PASS			

AND

The AND function is under the Excel Logical functions category. It is used to check if the specified condition in a test is TRUE. For instance, we can utilize the function to check if a number in a particular cell is less than 100 and greater than 50. The function is used in financial analysis to test multiple conditions. Aids in avoiding nested IFs, and can be used together with OR function.

Formula
=AND(logical1, [logical2], ...)
Here,
  o Logical1 – logical value or first condition to evaluate. Required argument.
  o Logical2 – logical value or second condition to evaluate. Optional argument.

Example
Simple AND function demonstration. The AND function checks to make sure that all arguments are TRUE, if any argument evaluates to FALSE, it will return FALSE.

D4				f_x	=AND(A4>0, A4<B4)

⊿	A	B	C	D
1	AND Function			
2				
3	Data 1	Data 2	Formula	Result
4	4	9	AND(A4>0, A4<B4)	TRUE
5	4	9	AND(A5>0,A5>B5,B5>15)	FALSE
6	4	9	AND(A6<0,A6>B6,B6>15)	FALSE

Example using AND function and IF function

Assume we want to calculate the incentive for all salespersons in our company. To get a commission of 15%, they have to achieve sales greater than $4,000 in a year as well as achieve an account target of 3 accounts or higher.

D4				f_x	=IF(AND(B4>4000,C4>3),B4*15%,0)

⊿	A	B	C	D	E	F
1	IF AND Function					
2						
3	Salesperson	Total sales	Accounts	Commission		
4	Tom	3500	2	0		
5	Stephanie	4700	4	705		
6	Harry	5000	7	750		
7	Diane	5500	3	0		

- **XNPV and XIRR**
  These functions are a lifesaver to analysts especially those working in

financial planning & analysis, equity research, or investment banking.

XNPV

The XNPV function utilizes specific dates that matches every discounted cash flow in the series, while the regular NPV (Net Present Value) function immediately assumes all the times/dates are equal. Therefore, the XNPV function is much more accurate and should be utilized rather than the regular NPV function.

Formula
=XNPV(rate, cash_flows, date)
Here,
- o Rate – discount rate to be utilized throughout the period.
- o Values (cash flows) – range of numeric values that constitute the income and payments where:
  Positive values (positive cash flow) are regarded as income.
  Negative values (negative cash flow) are regarded as outgoing payments.

o Dates (of cash flows) – date ranges corresponding to a range of payments. The date range should have similar length as the values range.

Example

In the example below, the XNPV function is utilized to calculate the NPV of a sequence of cash flows that are based on specific dates.

Assuming:

o The discount rate is 8%.
o The start date is 30th of June 2018.
o Cash flows are gotten on the same date to which they correspond.
o The period between the specified start date and the specified first cash flow is six months.

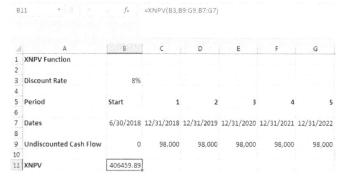

B11			f_x	=XNPV(B3,B9:G9,B7:G7)			
	A	B	C	D	E	F	G
1	XNPV Function						
2							
3	Discount Rate	8%					
4							
5	Period	Start	1	2	3	4	5
6							
7	Dates	6/30/2018	12/31/2018	12/31/2019	12/31/2020	12/31/2021	12/31/2022
8							
9	Undiscounted Cash Flow	0	98,000	98,000	98,000	98,000	98,000
10							
11	XNPV	406459.89					

From the above, the XNPV function returns $406,459.89 since XNPV recognizes that the period between the specified start date and the specified first cash flow is six months.

XIRR

The XIRR function is under the Excel financial functions category. It calculates the IRR (Internal Rate of Return) for a cash flows series that might not be periodic. It performs this by assigning precise dates to every individual cash flow. The core benefit of utilizing the XIRR function is that it can accurately model such randomly timed cash. The XIRR function is used in financial modeling to determine an investment's value or understand the practicality of a project without regular periodic cash flows. This function aids in understanding the rate of return received from an investment. Therefore, it is normally used in assessing and choosing between more than one investment.

Formula
=XIRR(values, dates,[guess])

Here,

- o Values – range of values representing the series of cash flows. Required argument.
- o Dates – series of dates corresponding to the specified values. Any additional dates must be later than the initial date, since the initial date is the beginning date and additional dates are future dates of income or outgoing payments. Required argument.
- o [guess] – initial estimate/guess of the IRR. If not provided, the default value will be 10%. Optional argument.

Excel utilizes an iterative technique to calculate XIRR. Making use of a changing rate (beginning with [guess]), XIRR cycles across the calculation until the outcome is accurate within 0.000001%.

Example
Assuming a project began on 1st of January 2018. The project provides cash flows during the middle of year one, after six months, at the end of – one and

half years, two years, three and half years, and annually thereafter.

	A	B	C	D	E	F
					=XIRR(B4:B9,A4:A9)	
1	XIRR Function					
2						
3	Date	Cashflow				
4	8/6/2018	-800				
5	8/8/2019	100				
6	8/12/2020	200		XIRR	19.52%	
7	8/6/2021	300				
8	8/6/2022	400				
9	8/1/2023	500				

From the above formula, the part for [guess] is blank, so Excel uses 10%, which is the default value. XIRR and XNPV are closely associated. The rate of return returned by XIRR is the same as the interest rate matching XNPV = 0.

Chapter 7

Excel Shortcuts

To be very productive, faster, and more competent when performing financial analysis or building financial models, it is vital to know the core keyboard shortcuts in Excel. It may appear slower in the beginning if you are used to working with the mouse, however it is worth the time and effort taken to learn these essential shortcuts. Below are the best timesaving shortcuts in Excel.

Formulas

Action	Shortcut
Examine part of a formula	F9
Toggle formulas off and on	Ctrl + `
Toggle relative and absolute formulas	F4
Autocomplete a function	Tab
Insert function arguments	Ctrl + Shift + A
Define Name (Opens Name Manager)	Ctrl + F3
Define name by making use of row and column labels	Ctrl +Shift +F3

Action	Shortcut
Paste name into a formula	F3
Calculate every worksheet in all the open workbooks	F9
Calculate active worksheet only	Shift + F9
Force calculation of all worksheets	Ctrl + Alt + f9
Autosum selected cells	Alt + =
Display the dialog box for function arguments	Ctrl + A
Collapse or expand the formula bar	Ctrl + Shift +U
Enter array formula	Ctrl Shift + Enter
Open the dialog box for Insert Function	Shift + F3

Formatting

Action	Shortcut
Apply number format	Ctrl + Shift + !
Apply percentage format	Ctrl + Shift + %
Apply general format	Ctrl + Shift + ~
Apply time format	Ctrl + Shift + @
Apply date format	Ctrl + Shift + #
Apply scientific	Ctrl + Shift + ^

Action	Shortcut
format	
Apply currency format	Ctrl + Shift + $
Italic	Ctrl + I
Bold	Ctrl + B
Display dialog box for Format Cells	Ctrl + 1
Decrease indent	Alt + H + 5
Increase indent	Alt + H + 6
Decrease decimal	Alt + H + 9
Increase decimal	Alt + H + O
Decrease font size	Alt + H + FK
Increase font size	Alt + H + FG
Align right	Alt + H + A + R
Align left	Alt + H + A + L
Align center	Alt + H + A + C

General

Action	Shortcut
Cut selected cells	Ctrl + X
Copy selected cells	Ctrl + C
Display the dialog box for Paste Special	Ctrl + Alt + V
Paste content from clipboard	Ctrl + V
Repeat last action (For instance if you just applied red fill	F4

Action	Shortcut
and a border to a single cell, you can utilize this shortcut to do the same formatting to more than one selected cells.	
Redo last action (allow several levels of redo's; every time you do this, Excel will move forward one level)	Ctrl + Y
Undo last action	Ctrl + Z
Display the dialog box for Find, with the Replace tab selected.	Ctrl + H
Display the Dialog box for Find and Replace	Ctrl + F
Find previous match	Ctrl + Shift + F4
Find next match	Shift + F4
Open help	F1
Open options	Alt + F + T
Insert column	Alt + I + C
Insert row	Alt + I + R
Insert worksheet	Shift + F11
Toggle references	F4

File

Action	Shortcut
Create new workbook	Ctrl + N
Open workbook	Ctrl + O
Save workbook	Ctrl + S
Save as	F12
Open print preview window	Ctrl + F2
Print file	Ctrl + P
Go to next workbook	Ctrl + Tab
Close current workbook	Ctrl + F4
Close Excel	Alt + F4

Selection

Action	Shortcut
Select all	Ctrl + A
Select entire column	Ctrl + Space
Select entire row	Shift + Space
Cancel selection	Esc
Add cells anywhere in the worksheet to the selection	Ctrl + Click
Extend current selection to adjacent cells	Shift + Click
Toggle add to selection mode	Shift + F8

Enter/Edit Data

Action	Shortcut
Fill right from the left cell	Ctrl + R
Fill down from the above cell	Ctrl + D
Enter and move left	Shift Tab
Enter and move right	Tab
Enter and move up	Shift + Enter
Enter and move down	Enter
Enter same data in several cells	Ctrl + Enter
Complete entry and remain in same cell	Ctrl + Enter
Cancel entry	Esc
Edit or insert comment	Shift + F2
Edit active cell	F2
Accept autocomplete suggestion	Tab
Go to end of cell contents	End
Go to start of cell contents	Home
Select within a cell	Shift + ← (or Shift + →)
Delete character to right	Delete
Delete character to left	Backspace

Chapter 8

Conclusion

Excel operates like a database, organized into columns (represented by letters) and rows (represented by numbers) that contain functions, formulas, and information used to execute complex calculations. It is mostly used as a calculator, to organize personal information, employee information, contact information, and financial data. In this book, we were able to go through the excel terms, operators, usage/application of formulas, usage/application of functions, basic and advanced functions, as well as shortcuts to help you become better at financial analysis and business modeling. Practicing and going along with the provided examples will help a lot towards achieving targeted goals in this journey.